A NEFARIOUS PENTAGRAM

by marie glen

CONTENTS :   Page:

CHAPTER ONE

THE 'END' IS NOT YET

When the first angelic mind began to ponder a different universe than God's, apocalypse began. And ever since Cain slew Abel, a nefarious, and ghostly edifice and potential has been slowly, but surely, taking shape in our world. Through the ages of civilization, this diabolical structure has been growing, block upon block, pentagram upon pentagram, with its final face being the crowning achievement, (the true conspiracy) and the shadowy results of millennia.

The "Book of Revelation" or

1

"Apocalypse" reveals this ghostly structure in a colorful and majestic vision which was seen and recorded by John the Apostle in his old age when he was banished to the uninhabited Island of Patmos. Dramatic events are portrayed in sequence and series like a symphony of visions upon a lavishly set stage.

Like thick velvet curtains slowly parting, "Apocalypse" reveals its secrets, and if we will settle back as if in ringside theater seats, we will soon hear a thunderous noise of approaching hoof beats. Four powerful and notorious horses, with riders, gallop steadily across the stage, stirring up clouds of dust and sand as they go. They are howling winds upon the stage of time. Our hair blows back from our faces, and sand stings our eyes and coats our teeth. They soon dwindle from our sight. But what we want to remember is these "Four Horsemen of the Apocalypse" once they begin their ride, continue their gallop throughout the whole (Revelation) production, with each gallop becoming more thunderous and pronounced at the 'end'. It is in their winds, that the rest of the Apocalypse visions occur.

Where may the world we live in be heading? Where might it be in fifty years or less from now? Peering through the mists of the future, what potentially awaits mankind?

3

Better than Nostradamus, more accurate than Edgar Cayce, the mysterious and infamous "Book of Revelation" is a window to the world of tomorrow, perhaps a world just around the corner, certainly a world whose foundations can be glimpsed today. It was written almost two thousand years ago, yet within its pages can be found the answers for today! For if we are able to read its warnings, perhaps we can apply the brakes, lest mankind rush quickly into the perils and cataclysms it so vividly portrays. To do this, we must understand its mysteriously cloaked message.

One of the intricate keys to reading this mystic message, is to realize, and fully understand, that all its visions play out to the utter end of the last act, each vision being like the musical note of a song, which once begun, continues to sound til the very end of the apocalyptic composition. The story is classic good versus evil, indeed it is the peak of good and evil, and a frozen moment and snapshot of it.

In this epic production, it's the bad guys who steal center stage. They didn't begin as villains. People built them, and contributed to them, with the best of intentions. But over time, they expand, and develop a life and essence all their own, until one day they are seen to all rear up with a mighty roar.

"Apocalypse" is the drama that flows out from them. Seeing them early, is our warning, and even though they are phantoms, they're easy to see if we realize they are the biggest influences which are working upon humanity and the world today. They begin, grow and endure. Everything runs its course, then suddenly, at the end of the vision, with a flourish, they're gone, and are replaced by a green and lush world of fruit filled trees and sparkling rivers, where "the lion will eat straw like the ox, and the bear will graze with the cow". [Isaiah 11:7]

The Revelation narrative, is a complete drama of the ages. It's the story of human history as a whole, the story of all peoples, and every nation, and it's the story of every individual. Like holding mirror up to mirror, producing the mirage of a long hallway – the many stories of life, are the one story, repeated over and over. And it's the lesson and drama being written upon every heart. But the revelation climax is not a set schedule. It can happen sooner, or later. It's a constant war, a war of good and evil.

CHAPTER TWO

NOTORIOUS HORSEMEN

In the prophetic theater of "Apocalypse" we see a scene in the starry heavens – a glorious and mighty throne is surrounded by flashes of lightning, smoke and huge, heavenly creatures singing "holy, holy, holy" along with myriads of winged angels as far as the eye can see. We watch, as the Lamb of God, the Lord, the only Begotten, is given a rolled up scroll. This is a long scroll, rolled and bound with a series of "seven seals" with the first seal being visible, for it closes, like a sticker, the end of the scroll. Each seal will be broken, allowing portions of the scroll to be unrolled and progressively read. It is when the Lamb breaks open the first seal, that the Revelation story truly begins. [Rev 5:1-7; 6:1]

The four horsemen we saw galloping, are the first four seals on this scroll. They are galloping, because their influence is on the gallop. That is to say, they increase. Each one, along with the rest of the seven seals, are seven advancing elements, which gallop and pick up momentum through the latter age, the latter age being the years of our Lord, A.D.

When with dramatic, and heavenly fanfare, the Lamb breaks the first seal, an angel cries "Come!" and the first horseman of the apocalypse comes riding

out upon the wide expanse of the earth.

He is upon a white horse, and he is given

a crown and a bow, and he goes out

conquering and to conquer. [This one is

said to have a twin, a shadow, a fifth

horseman if you will.] This conqueror

began his gallop, at the dawning of the

age (of our Lord A.D.) as the spreading

gospel of our Lord and Savior. It changed

a large slice of the world, even becoming

a world! Conquering the old 'gods' and

"triumphing openly over them".

[Colossians 2:15] This horse and rider is

unique, in that almost from the beginning

of his ride, he *has* had a parallel rider,

who gallops alongside him throughout the

age, and then accelerates toward the 'end' right along with him, even overshadowing him! The parallel rider of course is a counterfeit gospel, one which is reborn into the world "coming in unawares", or what we today would call, "on the sly". [Jude 4]

This scroll of seven seals is the revelation narrative. And remember! Each seal, and every vision within them, and vision within vision, play out til the 'end' like an increasing crescendo of them all. This is in the same manner in which each of the four horsemen of the apocalypse, once they begin to ride, continue their gallop right to the end of the age. [Rev 6:1,2]

11

Meanwhile, back in the starry expanse of the heavens, the second seal on the scroll is broken, and more of the scroll is unrolled. An angel cries "Come!" and a second rider comes forth, sitting upon a galloping red horse, its hoofs, stirring up the dust of time. This horse and rider "has power to take peace from the earth". And he has, during this age, and all ages, for this one is "war". And "war" has been mankind's constant unwanted companion. The red horse's rider is "given a great sword" for his weaponry has been a growing pageant (also). Some bible translations say of this red horse and rider called war – "he is given a long sword". [Rev 6:3,4]

At the third seal's opening, the third horse to appear upon Earth's scene, is a black horse. And this rider has a scale or "balance" in his hands. In the heavens, a voice sounds from among the four majestic "living creatures", which are seen at the sides of the throne of God, and the voice says, "a measure of wheat for a day's wages.. and a day's wages for a measure of barley, but don't hurt the oil or the wine." The increasingly complex *scale and balance* of "mercantilism" and trade, has steadily grown and taken root throughout the ages of man. But because of "war" (and man's imperfections) there has been, is, and will be, shortage, imbalance, and even famine. [Rev 6:5,6]

When the Lamb of God breaks the fourth seal and unrolls more of the scroll, a voice cries out once again, "Come!" And out comes a ("bruised" and) pale horse, the fourth horse of the apocalypse. This rider has a name! And his name is "death" and "the grave follows him closely". Most bible translations say, "and *hell* follows him closely". But a closer translation to the *original language used*, is "*the grave*". And this includes the mass grave wherever and everywhere it appears. For this horseman is said to claim a quarter of the earth "by sword, famine, plague, pestilence" (including chemical) "and with the wild beasts" or predators (killers) "of the earth". This horse and rider, also, continue their gallop and growth to the end, with an escalation toward the conclusion. [Rev 6:7,8]

So we see four threads which contribute to the tapestry of the Lord's years A.D. – the first, the conqueror, then war, famine and mass graves. These four are the well known and notorious "Four Horsemen of the Apocalypse" and are the first four seals of the "Seven Sealed Scroll" which is, the revelation narrative.

When the Lamb breaks open the fifth seal, John, who is the one who witnesses and writes down these visions, sees a vision "at the foot of the altar". He sees "the souls of those murdered for the Word of God, and they cry out with a load voice,

'When O Lord, Holy and True will you avenge our blood upon the earth?' They are given white robes and told to 'rest and wait patiently' until the remainder of the number of those who will be killed as they were, is complete". This "crying out" is like the blood of Abel, whom Cain slew, which "called to God from the dust of the earth". This seal is persecutions. It is present during the age, and accelerates. [Rev 6:9-11; 1; Thess 4:13,14; Gen 4:10]

Like a mighty trumpet blast, the opening of the sixth seal, is the releasing of a great cataclysm! In a dramatic flourish, one curtain closes... and another opens. [Rev 6:12]

16

CHAPTER THREE

SERPENTS AND WIZARDS

As we look through and adjust the lens of the Book of Apocalypse, we can bring into focus five main characters. They are the pentagram. Before we get better acquainted with each individual point of this pentagram, let's first look at this whole cast of special characters – the Big Beast, the Little Beast, the Global Harlot, the False Prophet, and the shadowy enigma called Mystery Babble.

Cast member number one, a many scaled and hairy, large beast, like a dragon, rises from turbulent seas, and becomes a world beast. The second character, the small beast, like a lamb, stands upon open land. The third character, called a harlot, is scantily clad in purple and gold, as she helps pull the wool over the eyes of all the world. The false prophet is a great wonder working wizard. And mystery babble is the potion, spell, and powerful concoction which is distilled upon the world. [Apoc/Rev 13:1-10; 13:11-18; 19:20; 17:18; 17:5]

The writhing intrigues of these five, become the body of the serpent, a five pointed pentagram, which will come to cover the earth like a wet, heavy quilt set low in the atmosphere, smothering the

18

very air and breath of humanity. This quilt is the revelation pentagram. It's worth repeating, and tragically ironic, that most of it is built and maintained by very well meaning hands and well intentioned souls. But not only do all five change, by being passed through many human hands, but hidden spiritual forces work very hard to influence them. These five characters, are forces in the world, described in Apocalypse, as they are in final days, in their final guise and costumes. It is this guise we are looking for. The roots of the world beast, the little beast, the harlot, the wizard and mystery babble, can be spied in the world around us. We can see them now, as trends. These five corners of the pentagram are like interlocking

building blocks. The structure they are

forming today is different from any other

pentagram which has stood in the world of

yesteryear.

CHAPTER FOUR

DREAMS, VISIONS

AND PENTAGRAMMATION

The world beast, has stood twice in the world before. The first time it was two versions of the same thing, with one version following another, inquisitions following persecution. And once again, our clue is the same, two of one pattern, but this time it's first appearance was very brief. And the little beast (the 'Caesars') didn't so much arise within it, but were inventor and dreamer of it (a head which expired). Its first modern form faded in barely a shuttering breath, but then it rose anew.

Meanwhile, the wizard had used his mighty wand to change the world into a new world, for he has mesmerized the world, and thrown it into the arms and alleys of the harlot who is openly and shamelessly in bed with kings and politicians. [Rev. 17:2]

Seeking to become sole judge, is the recesses and hallways of her "forehead" – the throne and power of the enemy, the foaming elixir of mystery babble, which is every untruth, and all false ideas and delusions. [Apoc/Rev 13:1-10; 13:11-18; 19:20; 17:18; 17:5]

If we wade into the obscure waters of bible prophecy, we will find ourselves washing up upon shores sporting fresh Roman columns. After all, look how large a part of the modern world was built upon the classic Roman and Greek worlds before us.

Also prominent upon the bible prophecy stage, is Daniel the prophet. He too, is a pillar of bible prophecy. His book in the Old Testament helps us to decipher the Book of Revelation! The visions and dreams he recorded, vividly show us our first and very important character of the pentagram, the latter day world beast or body. In his ancient writings, we find columns of today, which evolved straight from Rome.

In Daniel's day (Dn 2) Israel had been

captured, and Daniel, with many of the rest of his nation, was "in captivity" at Babylon – until Cyrus, an exact prophesied number of years later – ruling over Babylonia (all Babylon and Assyria) told all Daniel's people, the Hebrews, "in all his lands – you may go home." [Ezra 1:1-3]

Ruling over Babylon, at the time of Daniel and Israel's captivity, was mighty King Nebuchadnezzar. One night the king had a disturbing and very troubling dream. Yet even though his heart and mind were fearfully haunted by the dream, King Nebuchadnezzar couldn't remember it! So he threatened to kill the wise men of the court, unless one of them

24

could tell him, not only the interpretation of the dream, but the dream itself! Of course none of the king's wise men could tell him the dream, or the meaning of the dream, but young Daniel, who had risen to become an important member of the king's court, said,

"Wait!" (Don't kill anybody!) "I'll tell you the dream and its meaning! Let me pray to my God, and I'll tell you tomorrow." [Dan 2:1-16]

Daniel came back the next day and revealed that God had given the dream to King Nebuchadnezzar as an illustration of things to come in the course of the history of man's world. As a result of Daniel's knowing the dream, the court of wise men was spared. [Dan 2:24]

King Nebuchadnezzar had dreamt of a huge overshadowing statue. That was the whole dream! Just a huge statue, standing on the plains of Mesopotamia... It stirs memories of mankind's mysterious first tower and pyramid, the spiraling red brick "Tower of Babel" which rose through the mists of primordial time, its great swirling stairs meant for climbing upward, in order to look to, and reach to, the stars... King Nebuchadnezzar's imposing dream statue, simply adds detail to this tower and edifice of man.

As the first tower (of all men's towers) and as King Nebuchadnezzar's dream statue, it filled sky and earth, and even time, for it casts a long shadow. The

hands of man built it. But man's dream,

no matter how fine, noble or lofty,

because it stands alone, divorced from

God (the *very* spark and breath of *life*) can

only ultimately collapse, falling to earth in

a mighty resounding crash. [Dan 2:31;

Gen 11:1-4; Rev 18:2,9,14,15,19]

Nebuchadnezzar's fearsome dream

statue, Daniel said, and wrote, represents

unfolding world history. The statue was

made up of different sections. It had a

glowing head of gold - shimmering silver

shoulders and arms - a mighty bronze

torso - iron legs - and iron mixed with

clay, feet and toes. Each metal of the

statue, Daniel told the king, represents

27

the time of a mighty world empire and kingdom. Think of the Olympic medals, gold, silver and bronze (head, shoulders, torso). And how the bronze age was followed by the iron (which is the legs and half of the toes and feet). Daniel told the impatient king, the first, the head of the statue made of gold, was King Nebuchadnezzar himself! And his mighty kingdom of Babylon. The rest of the empires which followed, and were described by Daniel, can be seen (now) by looking back through history. Most bible scholars agree as to their identities.

This dream and vision, given by God, describes civilization's history as being built around the nation of Israel. To say there were other thriving civilizations and empires besides these of the statue, is a great understatement, but they aren't highlighted in bible history until the feet and toes, when the affairs and philosophies of all nations come together in the 'last' days. And then, still later, when all nations rejoice together in a world made new. [Dan 2:32,33,36-41; Rev 21, 22]

Nebuchadnezzar's dream statue is a history lesson, with Israel being center stage, for Israel's history is a microcosm of world history. Each of the world empires of Nebuchadnezzar's statue have been dramatically involved with Israel's history. After golden Babylon, came the dominion of silver Persia, or Media-Persia as it was called. Then there was the robust and galloping bronze Greece, followed by the iron of Rome (those great iron columns of Rome). And finally, the last global empire (of man) will be the iron and clay feet (and toes) which in the dream of King Nebuchadnezzar, Jesus strikes, thereby toppling the entire statue, and causing the dust of it to blow away upon the winds, never to be an oppression or burden upon the back of man again. [Dan 2:34,35]

Ancient King Nebuchadnezzar's dream was given to him by God [Dan 2:28]. And it is not only a perfect outline of history, but also reveals the foundation of the revelation pentagram. Gold equals Babylon; silver equals Persia; bronze was Greece, and the iron is Rome. They have evolved into today's world, and they are prominent upon the rich and flamboyant set of Apocalypse.

Not long after King Nebuchadnezzar's dream, Daniel had a dream of his own. In his dream, each of these empires of the statue, are described as great and terrible beasts. In chapter seven, beginning at verse one, we are told how Daniel "as he lay on his bed" dreamt of "four great beasts", which rose up out of the "stirring waters of the sea". [Dan 7:1-3]

These "four beasts" stand right alongside Nebuchaddnezzar's dream

31

statue, for Daniel's vision complements King Nebuchadnezzar's dream. In Daniel's vision, we see a first beast, a mighty lion, rise up out of the waves of the ocean, and leap upon the shore. His wet shaggy mane declares him king. But this one has "wings like an eagle's wings". This beast, and first empire, is Babylon. So we can say, this is a great golden lion, with large wings, like eagle wings. But in the vision, "the wings are plucked off, and the lion is made to stand as a man". The empire was humbled and lost its great luster. Yet the final empire in the Book of Revelation is called Babylon, and also refers to gold. It's been said that Babylon was the first truly monetary kingdom. [Dan 7:4]

The "second beast", and world empire, we see arise in Daniel's dream and upon the sands of time, is a great (silver) bear, "with one side raised up higher, than the other". It was called Media-Persia, but now we remember mostly "one side", glittery Persia, magical and mystical, but in reality, also a bear of a predator, which cast a threefold shadow upon the world, for it had "three ribs in its mouth" having subdued, and with iron fist, ruled three lands, mighty Egypt, fertile Babylonia and between the two, the land of the Hebrew tribes along the sapphire waters of the ever popular Mediterranean. [Dan 7:5]

The "third beast" of Daniel's vision, is a large, pouncing, (bronze and) spotted leopard. But this leopard has two sets of wings! And four heads! Greece's youthful Alexander the Great, was lightning quick (as with four wings) in subduing vast territories. The leopard's four heads, are the four divisions of Alexander's Empire, after he died of fever at a young age. Yet also these four heads surely reveal Greece's great love for the pursuits of the human mind – philosophy, education, oration and lecturing, and the arts and theater. It's not hard to see the bronze of Greece in our own world of today. [Dan 7:6]

Another theory sees these three beasts as representing kingdoms influencing Israel much closer to our own day (the

British lion, Russian bear, and German leopard). Both theories hold true, as prophecy is a repeating pattern. (Even if yesterday's nefarious pentagram, is not the same as tomorrow's nefarious pentagram.) It is also true that most, if not all, Bible prophecy is at the very least, dual, having a fulfillment of its own day, called an 'immediate' fulfillment, and a fulfillment in the 'last' days, called an 'end' of days fulfillment and final apocalypse.

The fourth and final beast of Daniel's dream vision is worse and "more terrible" than the lion (of gold), the (silver) bear, and the (bronze) leopard. This beast has ten horns, and it's not likened to an animal, but is described as more closely resembling a scaley, fire breathing dragon! One with iron teeth. It eventually absorbs all the world, becoming truly global, for it "devours the nations with its great iron teeth". These iron teeth or columns of Rome, are its politics, senates, courts, debates and architecture. These columns abide and evolve and eventually *give birth* to the world beast John sees rising in the vision called "Revelation". A beast for John's day, and an evolved beast for latter days. [Dan 7:7,19,(20-22); Rev 13:1]

This great "most terrible" beast, of Daniel's dream, besides "iron" teeth, has ten horns, and "bronze" claws. With its bronze claws, it "tears up the residue".

That is to say, the bronze claws break up the residue (not devoured by the iron teeth) and scatters it like dust. All nations lose their identities under the pervasive influence of the bronze. [Daniel 7:7,19]

We find this world beast of iron and bronze (roman/graeco) and ten horns, at the beginning of Revelation, chapter thirteen, and in chapter seventeen, where it's revealed that the beast turns red. Its ten horns are given crowns. And they are ten "kings which rule one" (final) "hour with the" (world) "beast.." And up steps another one, an eleventh, also of the world beast, a "little horn. He's our second cast member of Apocalypse, a second corner of the apocalyptic pentagram, called a *little beast*. It is said of this one (a final caesar) that he rises or appears "upon the wing of abominations" (most terrible) and (he too) "works abomination" [Dan 9:27, NASB and Amplified Bible; Rev 13:1, 11-18; 17:3].

Unlike the world beast, the wizard, the global harlot, and mystery babble, the little beast is a man! His influence is said to be for three years and six months, after which, the Ancient of Days will close the books and the Son of Man will return on the clouds. Daniel was told to close his book and take heart. These beasts would walk the earth in an age and days later than his own. [Dan 9:27; 7:13,14]

CHAPTER FIVE

FANCY FOOTWORK

As the Lamb of God unrolled the scroll
he holds, the Four Horsemen of the
Apocalypse, Conqueror, War, Famine and
Death, began their gallops, and a fifth seal
was opened, showing an abyss where the
blood of murdered ones are crying out to
God. Opening the sixth seal (which is the
sixth chapter of the Book of Revelation /
Apocalypse) is an explosive event. It's
something new. The world has never seen
the likes of it before. It not only explodes
mightily upon the scene, but has a great
mushrooming effect, for it becomes

something which changes much of the very fabric of life. John tells us, that when the Lamb of God reveals the sixth seal, everything goes black. The earth shakes as it never has before, and both the sun and moon are hidden. The moon becomes red, and the sun black. This indeed sounds ominous. It seems the only (and much needed) ray of light is – "He who sits on the Throne, shall spread His Tabernacle" His presence, over those who "worship at His Throne, both day and night. They shall not hunger, nor thirst, nor shall the sun or heat smite them, or beat down upon them, for the Lamb in the center of the Throne shall lead them to springs of living" (fresh) "water".

The opening of the sixth seal,

unleashes a great (new) wind. One that

makes the very stars quake in the

heavens. Thick clouds roll in, covering the

sky. Something so explosively new occurs,

that there is an accompanying great

spiritual earthquake which builds and

builds, until the very 'end' when "every

mountain and island of the planet is

moved from their place" and the kings and

generals, and even the everyday people,

will take to the caves and the rocks (and

the shelters) saying "who shall save us

from the presence of the One who sits on

the Throne and from the anger of the

Lamb, for the great day is come, and who

will save us?" Of course, these extremes

happen at the very end, although, if you will remember, there were many shelters built following the opening of atomic weaponry at the 1945 bombing of Hiroshima and Nagasaki. [Rev 6:12-16]

There's a strange, unnoticed twist here. Because these seals are galloping, progressing and increasing elements of the entire age, they are described here (in Revelation chapter six) both as they are at their beginning, or opening, but also as they are at the 'end' – in their full blown progression, at the very 'end of days'. Therefore events which occur extremely late upon planet earth, are described here, very early in the revelation narrative. This elaborate footwork seems to serve as a lock, hiding and disguising some of the vision "for many days".

After all this, we see four tall and mighty angels, standing at the four corners of the earth "holding back the wind" for a time, from blowing upon the earth, sea, or upon any tree. And the angels holding back the wind, say, "do not harm the earth, or the sea, or the trees, until we have sealed the servants of our God on their foreheads". [Rev 7:1-3]

While the new winds are being held back, and before the breaking of the seventh seal, angels of the Living God are sent out throughout the length and breadth of the Earth with a great seal and stamp of God. They have been instructed

43

to "seal the servants of God on their forehead". The ones receiving this illumination of clarity, are numbered in the twelve tribes of Israel. [Rev ch 7]

There's another seal and stamp upon those who are saved, the "seal of God" upon the heart. The heart is struck, whether quickly, or over time, as with a great sword of light, filling the heart with the very Spirit and Essence of God. This is what causes the heart to cry, "Father! My Father!" This cry of the heart is the "proof and guarantee" that we are His. It is the "pledge, promise and down payment of all that is to come and has been promised." [2 Cor 1:20-22; Romans 8:15,16]

After this, we see a great crowd, a

multitude too great to count, from every

tribe and people and tongue, and they are

now worshiping before the throne, both

day and night. [Rev ch 7]

When the Lamb of God breaks the

seventh seal, there is silence in heaven,

for about half an hour. [Rev 8:1]

CHAPTER SIX

FLAMES OF LIONS AND LOCUSTS

At the opening of the seventh seal, we see a line in the panorama of the starry heavens – seven angels having "Seven Trumpets". Another mighty angel approaches the throne of God. He gathers the prayers of all God's people and he mixes them with incense, which he takes from the altar which is in front of the throne. Then he throws this mixture to earth, and there is earthquake, and thunder and lightning. [Rev 8:1-6]

When the first of the waiting seven angels, sounds his trumpet, there is fire

46

and hail (or what appears to be hail). And all green grass, and one third of the earth and one third of all trees are burned up.

When the second angel sounds his trumpet, something resembling a great mountain falls *into the sea*, and one third of the creatures in the sea die. And fully one third of all trade is destroyed. [Rev 8:7,8]

The third trumpet is sounded, and a star called "Wormwood" falls on one third of the rivers and springs, and they become bitter.

When the fourth angel blows the fourth trumpet, a third of the sun, a third of the moon, and a third of the stars are smitten, causing day and night to be darkened by one third. [Rev 8:10-12]

Next, all is quiet. And we see a solitary
eagle. He dips and glides across the sky.
He soars and rises. And he cries out a
warning – "woe, woe, woe, because of the
three trumpet blasts which are to come".
This flight of a lone eagle across the
firmament, is like a cosmic outline written
across the sky. It separates the previous
teutonic and dramatic ecological woes
from the three woes which follow. [Rev
8:13]

When the fifth trumpet is blown, we
see a star (like a streak) fall to the earth.
This star is given the key to the
bottomless pit, called "the abyss". This is
called "a first woe". [Rev 9:1]

It's important for us to understand, that from the very beginning, God has done all things perfectly. For He Himself, can only be Perfection (or He too could not endure). The end result of all these things, can only be the very best end result possible. God knew what a bad turn creation would take, but He endowed man and angel with the ability to think, and thus choose, anyway! After all, it's far more likely He's creating a family (and an unbreakable paradise) than an ant farm.

The "Tree of the Knowing of Good and Evil" was openly displayed in the garden, for once thinking ability was given, a whole new world (or tree) of possibilities 'came to be'. And God, only able to be true, wasn't about to hide the truth, so there the tree was, in the original garden of life, which was Eden. [Gen 1:31; 2:9]

The "abyss" or bottomless pit, dear reader, is in us. It's inside every heart of every rational creature. For once imperfection starts, there is no end to the possible depths it can fall to.

When the angel opens this bottomless pit, the lone eagle cries "woe, woe, woe".

Dark, black smoke rises out of the abyss. And out of this smoke, and over a dark, dry and smoky landscape, come what (to ancient John) resemble locusts, "whirring locusts" at least one bible version says. These likely swarm and hover, as locusts are known to swarm and hover.

Power (Marshall Law?) is given to these and they torment mankind for five months by "stinging with fire", but they are not allowed (or are unable) to hurt any more plants or trees. [Rev 9:3,9]

The sixth angel blows the sixth trumpet, and four (dark) angels which were "bound at the great river Euphrates, and kept in readiness" for this hour, are unleashed. They destroy a third of mankind with their troops, who 'ride' horses with lion's heads, which shoot fire, smoke and sulphur from their mouths and tails. "This is the second woe." [Rev 9:13-19]

CHAPTER SEVEN

KALEIDOSCOPE

One of the final acts of Apocalypse, is the seventh trumpet. The seventh trumpet is the third woe. Within the sounding of the seventh trumpet, is "Seven Bowls", or "Vials", of final retribution. They are the final results and consequences, of all choices made since Eden, and by angels even before Eden.

Just as the seven trumpets, are the seventh seal, these seven vials, are the seventh trumpet.

But just when we thought we were starting to understand what's going on in this prophesying, and before the seven

vials or bowls of God are described, there

are five inserts. These inserts are dramatic

and grab our attention. They are like

boxed inserts we see in magazines and

history books. They are there to offer lots

of important information and insight. An

example of an earlier bible insert, is in the

Book of Genesis. In the first chapter, the

creation of man and woman is listed with

the rest of the acts of creation.. of the

sun, moon, and stars, and so on. But a

much more detailed version is given in

chapter two. The second, more detailed

account of the creation of Adam and Eve,

in chapter two, is an insert to the creation

list in chapter one.

The five inserts in the Book of Revelation, are placed between the sixth trumpet, and the sounding and occurrences of the seventh trumpet. They are another example of an intricate pirouette, designed to camouflage the message of Apocalypse "for a time".

* * *

Mighty curtains open upon a blue sky. And we see a strong angel who is "coming down from the heavens". He is surrounded by a cloud, and has a rainbow upon his head. His face is like the sun, and his feet are like mighty pillars of burning fire. In his hand, he holds a "little book" which is open. He places his right foot upon the sea, and his left foot upon the land. When

54

he speaks, his voice is like a roaring lion, and seven peals of thunder speak too. John is about to write what they have uttered, but a voice from heaven says "seal up what the seven thunders spoke and do not write it". The angel standing on land and sea, lifts up his right hand to heaven, and swears by Him, who lives forever and ever, and who created heaven and earth, and the sea, and all things therein, saying, "henceforth there will be no more delay, but in the day of the voice of the seventh angel, when he is about to sound the seventh trumpet, the mystery of God is finished, even as He revealed to His servants the prophets". A voice from heaven tells John to take the little book from the hand of the strong angel, who hands him the book saying, "Take and eat it. In your mouth it will be sweet as honey, but in your stomach it will be bitter" (a bitter pill). "You must prophecy again! Concerning many peoples, nations, tongues and kings". [Rev ch 10]

Next, in a second mini-act, John is given a measuring stick and he is told to go and measure the temple and the altar, and the people who worship therein, but he's to leave out the courtyard, for "the nations" will trample it under their feet for three and a half years, the years being Hebrew years which are twelve months, of thirty days, with a leap month about every three years. During the three and a half years, two witnesses of God prophesy in the city (of the sanctuary). They will wear 'sackcloth' and are reputed to be able to control weather, and strike anyone trying to harm them during the three and a half years. But the large beast (and that) which comes up out of the abyss, will kill them, and their dead bodies will be left lying in the street for three and a half days while the nations rejoice, and send gifts to one another in celebration, for these two were a major annoyance to the world. Then while all nations watch, the breath of life re-enters the two witnesses, they stand upon their feet, are summoned by a voice, and taken up to heaven in a cloud. At that very hour, there is a great earthquake which kills seven thousand, and a tenth of the city falls. And now we hear the angel say, "The second woe is past" (of lions with brimstone) "behold the third woe comes quickly." For the seventh angel is about to sound his trumpet. [Rev 11:1-14]

When the seventh and last trumpet is sounded, there are loud voices in heaven which proclaim – "The kingdom of the world is become the kingdom of our LORD, and of His Christ, and He will reign forever and ever". And there is lightning, thunder, earthquake and hail/(debris?). [Rev 11:15-19]

CHAPTER EIGHT

SUN, MOON AND TWELVE STARS

The curtains of our third mini-act and insert open upon the portrayal of a whole history! Instead of beginning in the garden of Eden, or beginning with the four horsemen of the apocalypse, this history begins with the nation of Israel. The scene (Revelation chapter twelve) opens with "a great sign, a woman in heaven..."

In history, the mantle of (ultimate) truth is first (and last) worn by Israel, portrayed here as a woman "clothed with the sun, with the moon under her feet, and a circle of *twelve* stars around her

59

head". She is in labor *to give birth*. Then
we see a red dragon, having ten horns
and seven heads. He has "dragged a third
of the stars" (angels) "down from
heaven". He stands in front of the woman,
making ready to devour her child, called
the "man-child" as soon as he is born. The
great red dragon (history tells us) within
the person of Herod, had all the youngest
male children of Bethlehem "slain with the
sword" trying to kill the "man-child",
who's general time of birth, thus age, had
been pinpointed for him by the
unsuspecting three wise men as they
traveled through the land in search of a
new born King in the town of Bethlehem.
Herod had learned the name of the

60

prophesied town by consulting spiritual
leaders in Jerusalem.

But the woman safely gives birth to
the man-child (also called the Son of man)
"who is to rule all nations with a staff of
iron" [a cross-reference with Psalm 2:7,8].
His staff, or rod (a measuring stick or
rule) is iron, because truth is unbreakable.
The man-child (or Son of man) is "caught
up to God, and to His Throne" [vs 5]
where He now sits "at the right hand of
God". [Hebrews 1:3]

The dragon was foiled! Now the
woman (the early church) fled from the
dragon's resulting wrath, to a place which
was prepared for her, where she is to be
"nourished" for a time (a thousand two

hundred and sixty 'days').

The dragon raged, and Jerusalem was razed in extreme violence, in 70 A.D., scattering ancient Israel throughout the world, and also scattering the new Christians, and Christianity, largely into Europe, where it was planted, nourished and flourished (albeit amid persecutions and troubles) for a time – a first migration. [Rev 12:1-6]

After all this, the dragon thought he would march right up into the heavens, just as he always had. But after the man-child's life, death and resurrection, something had changed, a new territorial line had been drawn, and there was "fierce war in heaven". Michael and his angels fought, and the dragon and his one third of the angels fought. But like lightning striking, half the victory has been lawfully won! And they were cast out of heaven. When the dragon discovered himself no longer having access to the heavens, in great wrath, he once again pursued the woman! And he fiercely persecuted her (with great persecutions, inquisitions and perils). But the woman is given the two wings of a great eagle, that she may fly away, and be safe from the face of the dragon, for three (modern) divisions of time, and half a time.

After fierce dragon-like persecutions, Christianity did indeed migrate a second time, by sprouting eagle wings, and sailing to a new land. The year of 1620 is engraved upon Plymouth Rock where she landed. She is "kept safe from the fierce face of the dragon for three times and a half" after which time, the serpent guise of the dragon, vomits a flood after her, trying to wash her away from the very face of the earth. [Rev 12:7-9,13-15]

Sixteen twenty, plus three hundred and fifty (three modern times, and half a time) brings us to nineteen seventy. Then there was a flood, a strong proliferation, a no longer hidden social phenomenon, that exploded, and changed culture like a new exploding Renaissance...

Before this flood and proliferation, you could even say, preparing the way for it,

64

was a "false prophet" perhaps the biggest one ever. This prophet was put into play, and had great impact. 'He' is a wizard of huge proportions, and his spell and magic is in the brew which he mixes up and distributes to the masses. This prophet began as a man, but became an idea and a philosophy, one which is still changing the world. He gives visions and legends. He is a wizard and a magician. This devout one, has put on, not a dark robe, but a white one. He is the one who opened the explosive sixth seal, because one of his concoctions is a fire he gave to the "little beast" in chapter six - [Rev 13:(12)13 and Rev 6:12]. And if that's not enough, he will bring about the miracle and modern wonder, of the 666 apparatus. There's no telling what dazzling wonders he will cook up next. [Rev 19:20; 13:13,17; 6:12; Eccles 10:13] He is, of course, of the pentagram, which is the 'revelation five' which is the five primary Book of Revelation cast members, the world beast, the little beast, the wizard, the global harlot, and mystery babble which is written on the harlot's forehead.

Because of the false prophet, the flood released out of the mouth of the serpent almost washes away the woman who had been given eagle's wings. But! Alas! "The earth itself, will help the woman of God!" For it will swallow the flood!

But this is a bitter pill, for here, surely, is the prophet Joel's dry and smoky day and the environmental catastrophes of the first four "Trumpets". Jesus gave a dire warning of all this, when He was going to be crucified. Some of the women of Jerusalem were weeping as he walked by, but He told them not to weep for Him, but for children's children, for "if they will do this" (crucify Him) "in a green leaf, *what will they do in a dry leaf*?" [Luke 23:28-31; Joel 1 and 2]

After the earth swallows the flood, the dragon "goes off in his wrath" to (earnestly) make war with the remainder of the woman's (other) children (Israel), who "have the Commandments of God,

67

and" (now, or by this time) "hold to the testimony of Jesus". This is an important development, for Jesus, weeping tears over Jerusalem had said, "you will not see me again until you" (Israel) "have said – blessed is He (Jesus) who comes in the name of the LORD". [Rev 12:16-16,17; Mt 23:39]

CHAPTER NINE

FAT MAN, LITTLE BOY,

AND RIDDLE 666

Meanwhile, in order to make war with
Israel, the remainder of the woman's
seed, and to make war with the saints, the
dragon stood upon the sand of the sea.
[Here's our fourth insert, and chapter 13.]
And a great beast (the pentagram's large
beast turned "red") with seven heads and
a circle of ten horns came up out of the
sea. We have witnessed this huge
"terrible" beast with a circle of crowns
before. He is the fourth beast in Daniel's
dream of four beasts, the last one "more

terrible" with great iron teeth (or columns). This last one, like a not so silent background, after absorbing the other three, has remained and evolved. For he is now described as being like a leopard! With bear's feet, and the mouth of a lion! And "it's the dragon which gives him his power, and a throne, and great authority". [Rev 13:1,2; Dan 7:7,19]

One of its heads expires, but like mythical Hydra, the head springs back up (is rebuilt). And the entire world will follow after the rebuilt and many headed (world) beast, saying, "who is like the beast? And who can make war with the it?" The world beast listening to the enchantments of the false prophet, came under his spell, and in dementia, he speaks with great arrogance, blaspheming (personally insulting) God and God's throne. The world beast or body, will make war with the saints. And he perseveres over them, and is given authority for forty-two months (or three and a half years) over every tribe, nation, tongue and people. All nations will be in alliance (or "accord") with 'him'. [Rev 13:3-8; Daniel 9:27 and Strong's Exhaustive Concordance, Hebrew word #1285 - "an accord, covenant or league"].

The second apocalyptic beast is soon revealed. And he stands on the seashore, having come up out of the earth. He has two horns, or seats of power. He is like a lamb, but in the end – he ends up speaking as a dragon. This "beast" has been called a "little horn" [Dan 7:8,21,22; 8:9-11] so he is a little beast, not a country or governing, but an office or seat of man, for the last verse in the chapter says "calculate his number.. it is the number of a man." He will say to the world, "worship the beast" (look to the world beast) "which was, then wasn't, and then was again". We're given a clue, in this thirteenth chapter of Revelation, to his identity. For he's the one who was given the capability of a new and different fire, which men saw as falling from the sky, convincing them to build up the world beast or body. And the little beast will (finally) give breath, and strength

(authority) to the world beast, its head,
now, back in place.

The final hours little beast (who has
two horns, sometimes nicknamed the
"little horn") is the one of which Daniel
said "upon the wing of abominations, shall
come one who abominates.. until a
complete destruction, one that is decreed,
is poured out on the one who desolates".
Remember, Jesus in Matthew, chapter
twenty-four said, "when you see the
abomination of desolation set-up in
Jerusalem, know that it is nigh." We've
got this man's number. It's the number of
a man, and it's 666. The last Caesar. And
he will set up an abomination and horrific
affront to God, known as 666. [Rev

13:11-18; 6:12-15; Dan 9:27; Mt
24:3,15]

The last Caesar (man-prince) will likely
be many different things, to many
different people – a religious leader, a
holy man, messiah, imam or prophet, a
political savior, a business redeemer, even
a long awaited E.T. 'foretold' by the false
prophet's philosophy, or even, by some –
hailed as Lucifer, bringing enlightenment
as he once claimed to do in Eden. [Rev
12:14]

CHAPTER TEN

A RED DRAGON ROARING

One day, as Jesus and His disciples were leaving the temple in Jerusalem, His disciples were marveling and pointing out the temple and temple buildings to Him, but He said,

"See all these? Truly I tell you, not one stone shall remain upon another which will not be torn down". [Mt 24:1,2]

Today all that remains of the temple and temple buildings Jesus was referring to, is the "Western Wall" or the "Wailing Wall" where worshipers come to offer daily sacrifices of prayers. But even the stones of this remaining wall, will one day be trampled, torn down and removed – for "not one stone shall remain upon another".

After the disciples asked Him about the time of His return, and the end of the age, He told them that an "abomination of desolation, spoken of by Daniel the Prophet" would be seen "standing in the Holy Place". ("Let the reader understand" says the scripture). [Mt 24:3,15]

In Daniel chapter nine, verses twenty-six and twenty-seven, the prophet said "Messiah will be cut off and have nothing" (i.e. He was executed on a cross as a criminal). "And the people of the prince" (the Caesars) "who is to come" (and most prophecy scholars agree this also refers to the last of men's princes) "will destroy the city and the sanctuary". Here, as between the two advents of Jesus, when our Lord came the first time, was buried and resurrected, and comes a second time at 'the end', there is a large time gap. But the scriptures, more times than not, speaks of the two advents in the same breath like a flowing continuum. So too with prophecy: the "city and sanctuary" was destroyed in 70 A.D., but is destroyed further, at 'the end'. For Daniel continues, "the end of it will come with a flood even to *the end*, there will be war, and desolations will occur. And he" (the 'prince') "will make a firm covenant

77

with the many, for one week". This is a *Hebrew* "week of years", or "seven years".

For a seven year term, there will be a declared world peace accord, covenant and league. "But in the midst" (or towards the middle) "of the week, he will put a stop to sacrifice and grain offering". [Dan 9:26,27]

"And on the wing of abominations, will come one who makes desolate even until utter destruction, the determined end, is poured out upon the one who makes desolate". [Dan 9:27]

Daniel further warns us, at the very end of his chapters – "From the time that the *daily sacrifice* shall be taken away" (stone by stone?) "and the abomination of desolation set up, there shall be three years and seven months" (don't forget, this is three and a half Hebrew years of thirty day months, plus a leap month). The verses actually word this as "one thousand, two hundred and ninety days". *Around the middle* of the seven year global agreement or term, Israel's "daily sacrifice" is stopped, taken away, or removed. According to Daniel, it is three years and seven months after this, that the abomination of desolation is set-up. [Dan 12:11,12 w/ 9:27]

Just as the world treaty is first broken with Israel, so too shall the desolating abomination first be set up in Israel, for as Jesus said, it will be seen "standing in the

Holy Place" (and that is THE sign to "take flight" - Matthew 24:16-31. This was also the sign remembered and heeded by the Christians of 70 A.D. when Jerusalem was razed. History records there was a pause, and the Christians seeing the banners of the gods of Rome at the corners of the Holy Temple quickly left the city, deeming this the abomination, and were spared.)

Here is how the verse reads, though this is paraphrased, and may even blend versions – verse eleven of Daniel chapter twelve – "From the time that the daily sacrifice is removed, and the abomination of desolation is set up, shall be three years and seven months." The next verse reads, "Happy is he who waits and comes to, the three years, eight and a half months later."

Here are both verses word for word – "From the time that the daily sacrifice shall be taken away, and the abomination that makes desolate is set up, there shall be a thousand two hundred and ninety days. Blessed is he who waits and comes to the thousand three hundred and thirty-five days" – (which is after forty-five additional days).

What dramatic thing will occur on that day? On the one thousand, three hundred and thirty-fifth day after the daily sacrifice is removed? And upon the forty fifth day after the "Abomination of Desolation" is "set up"?

Surely, we can come to no other conclusion, the abomination that desolates, is the 666 program, and it is set-up three years and seven months after "the daily sacrifice is removed" and brought to an end. The end of Revelation, chapter thirteen reveals it is set up by the little beast (the two horned last Caesar now "head" of the world beast) for he "causes all, the small and the great, the rich and the poor, to be given a mark on their right hand or forehead, and no one will be able to buy or sell except those who have the" (identifying) "mark, either the name of the beast or the number of his name. Here is wisdom, let him who has understanding calculate the number of the beast, for the number is that of a man; and his number is six hundred and sixty-six". Many believe this is John's code for his day, referring to Rome and Caesar, for the Roman numerals of the time, added together, equal six hundred and sixty-six. Rome persecuted the saints, fell, rose again, and persecuted, by inquisition, the saints again (or the dragon did, from both sides of the wars).

And in the same pattern of "was, and then wasn't, but then was again" it is also true of the final world body, in the repeating pattern of bible prophecy, it expired, but then it was again. [Rev 13:16-18,3]

As a possible first six, birth dates are

currently six numerals.

Later – after all these things have occurred – in Revelation twenty, verse four, we see "those who were *beheaded* because of their testimony of Jesus... and because they had *not* worshiped the beast or his image *or* received the mark on their forehead or on their hand, come to life and reign with Christ for a thousand years". This is a verse which shows us how the "mark of the beast" without which "no one can buy or sell" soon enough becomes a vehicle of killing and genocide. I say soon, for we know that forty-five days after the Desolating Abomination is "set up", those who have been able to wait it out, and come to the forty-fifth day are blessed. For Daniel, inspired by the Spirit of God, said "How blessed is he who keeps waiting and comes to the one thousand three hundred and thirty-five days" – Daniel 12:12. [The 666 program operates for forty-five days, until it is cut short by an intervening event upon the forty-fifth day of 666.]

Revelation 2:10 prophesies a "ten days of *tribulation*". Perhaps the last ten days of the forty-five days, are the most critical when upon day thirty-five it becomes policy that anyone found not having the identifying (locating? modifying?? chip?) 666, will be put to death. [See Luke 23:26-31.]

But blessed are those who make it to

the forty-fifth day!

Revelation 13:15, 16 and 17 says, "And it was given to" (the little beast) "to give breath" (and authority) "to the image" (or 'panel'?) "of the (world) beast, so that it can even speak" (i.e. has authority) "and it causes those who do not worship" (or swear allegiance to) "the image of the beast, to be killed. And he causes all, the small and the great, and the rich and the poor, and the free men and the slaves" (workers) "to be given a mark on their right hand or on their forehead" and (in those days) "only those who have the mark of the beast, either his name, or the number of his name, will be able to buy or sell".

"Happy the one who comes to the
forty-fifth day."

CHAPTER ELEVEN

OUTLINE IN THE FIRMAMENT

Now we see the curtain rise upon a new vision. This is the fifth and final insert, and its purpose is to summarize the Apocalypse. This act (or insert) is like watching four waves come washing into shore. John looks, and behold, the Lamb was standing on Mt Zion! And 'with' Him, are one hundred and forty-four thousand, having His name, and the name of His Father, written on their foreheads. Then John hears a voice from Heaven like the sound of many waters, and like the sound of thunder, and the voice which he hears is like the sound of harps. They sing a new song before the Throne, and no one can know the song unless purchased and redeemed from the earth. [Rev 14:1-3]

We look up, and like heavenly summations, we see "three angels" in sequence, fly across the firmament. The first angel has the eternal gospel to preach, saying to every nation, tribe, tongue and people,

"Worship God who made heaven and earth. Give glory to Him. For the hour of judgement is come."

A second angel cries "Fallen, fallen!" (crashed!) "is Babylon the Great" (the global harlot) "who has made all nations drink the wine of her fornications".

And a third angel follows, saying with a loud voice,

"If anyone worships the beast and his image, and receives his mark on his hand or forehead, he also will drink of the wrath of God mixed full strength" (the full results and apocalypse).

And a voice from heaven says to John, "Write! Blessed are the dead who die in the Lord from now on, for their deeds follow with them". It's so close to the very 'end' that their works quickly follow the (first) resurrection. [Rev 14:6-13]

Next, there is a twofold "harvest". We see sitting upon a white cloud, one like a Son of man. He has a golden crown on His head, and a sickle in His hand. An angel comes out of the Temple and yells to Him,

"Put in your sickle and reap the earth, for the fruit is ripe!" And He harvests the earth [Rev 14:14-16]. Matthew 24 says, "Immediately following the *tribulation* of those days.. they will see the Son of man coming on the clouds of the sky.. He will send forth His angels with a great TRUMPET, and they will gather His elect from one end under heaven to the other."

"In a moment, in the twinkling of an eye, at the last TRUMP, for the trumpet will sound and the dead will be raised, and we who remain will be changed." [1 Corinthians 15:52]. "In the days of the voice of the Seventh Trumpet, when it shall begin to sound, the mystery of God

91

shall be finished, as He has declared to His servants the prophets" [Revelation 10:7].

Then we see another angel come out of the Temple, and he has a sickle. An angel coming out from the altar, cries to him,

"Put in your sickle and gather the clusters from the vine of the earth, because her grapes are ripe!"

The Apocalypse vision is the story of the fullness of both *good* and *evil* (which is also *true* and *untrue*, and *Life* and *death*). The angel swings his sickle to the earth and "gathers" the clusters and throws them into the great wine press of God, and the wine press is trodden and blood (oil? like a great shadow?) comes out from the wine press, up to the horse's bridles, for a distance of two hundred miles. [Rev 14:17-20; Joel 3:14]

And thus do the inserts end, and we arrive at the commencement of the "Seven Bowls of God" – the Bowls or Vials, of the last seven plagues, which are within the seventh (and last) trump(et). [Rev 15:1]

CHAPTER TWELVE

IRON AND CLAY

The curtain closes. Although a seven

year accord had been triumphantly

ratified, and was celebrated as world

peace, and as the answer to man's dreams

and ideals, woefully, it isn't a very deep

peace. Daniel wrote – "the nations" or the

final day's (political and economic)

division of the nations, into the ten (iron

and clay) toes of Nebuchadnezzar's long

ago dream statue (or much later called

the ten horns and crowns of the beast)

"won't really cleave" to one another, being

some of iron (western) and some of clay

(not western).

Regardless of the world peace declared, soon after the environmental woes, the shortages, dryness and smoke of the first four Trumpets, old global and regional disputes flare back up into conflict. Our Lord included as a signpost, "there will be wars and rumors of war" because like the rest of the list of Mt 24 (Mk 10 & Lk 21) they escalate and increase towards the 'end'. These feuds cause more fires, thus more shortage, and more battles, and ever more smoke. And "out of the smoke" (of the abyss – remember the abyss?) come the (whirring) locusts which sting mankind with their tails (enforcing Marshall law) for five months. [Dan 9:27; Rev 9:3,9;

13:3,8; Dan 2:41-43; Joel 2:3; Mt 24:6]

Soon after this, within the sixth

trumpet, is when the two hundred million

troops, with 'lions' which shoot fire, smoke

and sulphur, sweep across the Euphrates,

killing one third. Six, sixty, six is

instituted, also within the sounding of the

sixth trumpet, and soon after, the nations

will "gather" to Armageddon, surrounding

Israel, for the last great battle and

conflagration of man. [Rev 9:2,3,9,16-19;

16:16; 2 Peter 3:10]

When the seventh trumpet begins to

sound, then the "mystery of God will be

finished" – "it is finished" Jesus said, as

He breathed His last mortal breath upon a

Roman cross. The possibilities of man's world may be cataclysmic, but his rescue was finished (almost) two thousand years ago. [Rev 10:7; 11:15; Jn 19:30]

The apocalyptic stage is cleared and the curtain closes. All is dark and quiet, but then the curtains slowly re-open upon a smoke filled, dry and dusty landscape. Against the dark gray firmament, there are seven angels, with seven vials (or bowls) of the last seven plagues. [Joel 1:15-20]

It is now things happen very "quickly". The seventh trumpet has sounded, and the seven bowls, within the seventh trumpet, are the final outcome of this whole drama, this whole world gone astray scenario. In the vision, these final vials are poured upon the land, the sea and the air.

Peter and Paul both wrote how the "Day of the LORD" (the day of trouble, when He returns "lest all be destroyed") will come unexpectedly, "like a thief in the night, in which the heavens will pass away with a great roar, and the elements will melt in fervent heat". It will begin, like a woman's labor pains, when the world is saying "peace! peace!". [2 Peter 3:10; 2 Thessalonians 5:2-4]

Second Thessalonians 1:7,8 tells us, "He comes with His angels" (to gather the elect, both living and dead) "and, with fire..."

These final seven plagues are poured
out very "quickly" if not concurrently. The
seven angels line up across the heavens
and the first bowl is poured upon the
earth, becoming a grievous sore or
contamination upon those unfortunate to
have the mark of the beast. The second
bowl is poured on the sea, turning it to
blood, and everything therein dies; the
third bowl is poured on the rivers and
springs of water, turning them to blood, to
which myriad angels say, "Righteous are
You, O Holy One, for they poured out the
blood of saints and prophets" (and
innocents) "and so you have given them
blood to drink". The fourth bowl is poured
upon the sun, and its heat scorches men.

The fifth bowl is poured upon the throne of the beast, and his kingdom goes completely dark, and they blaspheme and insult God on account of their pains and sores, but they do not repent of their deeds. The sixth bowl is poured on the Euphrates River, and it is dried up to make way for the kings of the east. For out of the mouth of the dragon, and out of the mouth of the (world) beast and out of the mouth of the false prophet (wizard) come three unclean spirits (lies, bitter) like frogs, for they are the spirits of demons, performing signs, which go out to the kings of the earth, to "gather" them to the last great battle, called Armageddon. The seventh bowl is poured on the air, and a loud voice comes out of the Temple, from the Throne, saying "It is done". And there is thunder and lightning, and a great earthquake greater than has ever been seen, and "the great city" falls, splitting into three parts, and "the cities of the nations fall".

Babylon the Great City, the final days, all encompassing ghost of Babel Tower – unyielding, built of bricks – is "remembered by God" for "her sins reach to" and challenge "the very heavens". She is given the "full cup of the wine of His fierce judgement; and every island and mountain flee, and a storm of huge (hail) stones falls upon man and they blaspheme God because of the hail." [Rev 15:1;

16:1-12,17-21]

An angel takes John to a desert, to a dry and barren place saying "Come with me, I will show you what happened to the Harlot, the Great City, Babylon, which sits on many waters. It's with her, the kings have committed fornication." (For the kings and politicians were in bed with her.) "And the inhabitants of the earth became drunk with her fornications" or, intoxicated and completely led astray by her indecencies. "Fornications" here, is translated from the Greek word "porneia", which means harlotry. And the word "harlot" is "porne" the feminine of "pornos" which is "to sell". [Rev 17:1,2; Strong's Greek #4204]

When the mists of vision clear, and we are shown for the first time a vision of this infamous "harlot". She is sitting atop the red beast, which has the seven heads, and ten horns with crowns, who is full of blasphemy and blasphemous names. She is decked out with silk, purple, scarlet, jewels, gold and pearls. She is drunk on the blood of the saints, and holds in her hand a golden cup full of "abominations", which are the "degrading and unclean things of her harlotry" and "pornos". It is a golden cup full of her abominations (her side-effects!) the abortions, murders, abductions, perversions, sex slave trade, and the dissolution of holiness and family and society. There's a time, before the hail

103

and debris of her crashing ("all the towers will fall") when God says "come out of her my people lest you too, have to drink down the full measure of the cup of her abominations". [Rev 17:3,4; 18:4]

"Upon the forehead of her" has been written Mystery Babylon The Great. Now at first glance we might underestimate this, thinking of it as a mere title. But, in comparison, the "Seal of God" on the foreheads of His own, isn't a mere title, but a "seal of ownership". And the seal itself is His Spirit. It infuses His people. [Rev 17:5]

The "forehead" contains one's thoughts and beliefs; the philosophy and psyche, one's attitude and world view. The world's forehead is Mystery Babble. Which is everything other than the "decree of God" (of Psalm 2) which is "the Son" and "all" things "being gathered into Him, whether on earth or in heaven" [Ephesians 1:10, KJ]. All men's philosophies and spiritual aspirations may even grow into a beautiful 'One World Faith' (heeding all religions minus one) which will be a magnificent dream, including the dream and aspiration of world peace, but man cannot go it alone.. "In the beginning, God." Apart from God, there is nothing.

John wonders greatly at this vision of the beastly woman! And the angel who showed him the harlot, says "Why are you marveling? I will tell you the mystery of the woman, and the mystery of the red beast she is being carried by".

Revelation 18:24 says she is guilty of all who have been slain upon earth - that would include since Cain slew Abel. Her forehead, which all have been a part of, is wrong belief, every lie, and all untruth. And, it is what is responsible for all these things of Apocalypse, and responsible for all sufferings upon the Earth. For untruth cannot stand. It can only crumble.

The World Beast having turned red, helped to carry the harlot, and the world, into dissolution and madness...

CHAPTER THIRTEEN

SOCIALISM AND CAPITALISM

"I will tell you the mystery of the (beastly) woman" says God's angel, "and the mystery of the beast with seven heads and ten horns. The seven heads are seven mountains" (continents, hills) "the woman is sitting on, and the ten horns are ten kings who have not yet received a kingdom, but they receive authority with the beast for one hour". (These are the ten divisions, the ten toes of Nebuchadnezzar's long ago dream statue.) "These ten kings have one purpose" (and one purpose only) "to give their power and authority to the (red) beast itself. These will make war with the Lamb, and the Lamb will overcome them because He is Lord of lords and King of kings!" [Rev 17:7,11-14]

"The waters which you saw where the harlot sits are people and multitudes and nations and tongues. And the ten horns (toes) and the (world) beast, will hate the harlot".

What's this?! They will hate the harlot?! The "world beast" or body, of ten divisions and kings, will hate the "harlot"?!

"They will make her desolate and naked, and will consume her flesh and devour her with fire. For God has put it in

108

their hearts to execute His purpose! To have a common purpose! to give their kingdom and reign to the (world) beast, until the words of God be fulfilled".

The angel of God tells us. "The woman whom you saw is the great city, which reigns over the kings of the earth." Surely this is a spiritual and global 'city' which plays the "harlot" (i.e. 'sex sells') – the city of man, which is all cities, its glaring lights, garish illuminations, and all her dark, lonely and dangerous streets, both actual and virtual. [Rev 15-18]

The great, heavy curtains of the apocalyptic stage quickly close and open anew, and we see an angel coming down who illumines the earth with his glory and cries out with a "mighty" voice, "Fallen!

Fallen! is Babylon the Great! She has

become a dwelling place of demons and

every unclean spirit, for all nations have

drank the wine of her immorality". The

kings are 'in bed' with her, and it's "the

merchants of the earth who have become

rich by her abundance of sensuality".

John heard another voice from heaven,

saying, "Come out of her my people, so

that you will not share her sins, and

receive of her plagues, for her sins have

piled up as high as heaven.." She shakes

her fist at the very heavens! "In one day,

her plagues shall come; pestilence,

mourning, and famine, and she will be

burned up with fire." [Rev 18:1-5]

The kings of the earth will lament
when they see from a distance, the smoke
of her burning, saying, "Woe, woe, the
great city Babylon, the strong city! For in
one hour your judgement has come." [Rev
9,10]

And "the merchants of the earth will
weep and moan because no one buys"
their fine lists of products anymore, all
manner of products and luxuries, the fine
cloths and ointments, fruits and rich
foods, chariots, and wagons, and the souls
and bodies of people. The sellers of these
things will weep and mourn saying, "Woe,
woe, the great city, for in one hour has
such great abundance been laid waste",
and all who trade.. were crying out as

they saw the smoke of her burning,

saying, "what city is like the great city?"

And they grieve, crying, "The great city, in

which all who trade.. became rich by her

wealth. In one hour she has been made

desolate" (in one hour, does her crash

occur). [Rev 18:11-19]

Another great angel takes up a stone

"like a great millstone" (a miller's stone)

"and threw it into the sea, saying - so will

Babylon fall and not be found anymore"

("rejoice over her o peoples! saints,

apostles and prophets"...) "never again

will the sound of musicians, harpists and

flutists be found in you city Babylon, or no

craftsman of whatever craft will be found

in you, nor shall the sound of the

millstone ever be heard in you again, nor any light in you, nor the voice of the bride or the groom; for your merchants were the great men of the earth and by your sorceries were all nations deceived" (by your charms and enchantments, all were led astray). [Rev 18:20-23]

One Passover day, when Jesus entered the Temple court, he heard a "babel" of activity, and found "those that sold oxen and sheep and doves, and the changers of money sitting". So He made "a whip of small cords and drove them all out, and poured out the changer's money and overturned their tables, and said to them that sold.. take these things away! And make not my Father's house a house of merchandise!" [John 2:14,15]. About Babylon the Great, Revelation 18:8 says, "In one day shall her plagues come, death, mourning and famine, and she shall be utterly burned with fire, for strong is the LORD God who judges her". She, like the table of the moneychangers at the entrance to the temple, will be swept away, and no longer will she sit on the backs of peoples and nations and tongues.

But what of the riddle of the World Beast or body, gone red, with its "ten kings"? Why do the beast and kings hate the harlot? Why do they desolate and consume her, and burn her with fire? Perhaps we can find the answer to this riddle, by looking closely at the world

114

around us. The five revelation characters stand big as you please. They are prominent, and prevalent. They are the largest forces at work upon humanity today. These two, the red beast with ten kings, or divisions; and the harlot – are socialism, and capitalism; or rather they are the very extremes of each. Socialism finally achieves its dream. It will devour capitalism. The red beast will consume the harlot city. The world beast (or body) which turned red, will consume capitalism (and its resources) it having embraced and turned to harlotry, and thus corruption of the world, to sell its goods.

After this vision, there is a great resounding chorus of heavenly voices, sounding like many waters, and thunder, saying, "Hallelujah.. Salvation and glory and power belong to our God, because His judgements are righteous and true. He has judged the great harlot who was corrupting the earth with her immorality, and He has avenged the blood of His servants upon her – Hallelujah.. Her smoke rises up forever and ever" (will be remembered always). The ever lasting lesson of knowing "good from evil" (life from death) will be deeply engraved upon every heart and mind. The choir of the heavenly angels continues, "Give praise to our God.. all you who revere Him, the small and the great. Hallelujah! For the LORD our God, the Almighty reigns. Let us rejoice and be glad and give glory to Him,

for the marriage of the Lamb is come and

His bride has made herself ready.." And

the angel who had showed John how

man's mighty Babylon falls, said, "Write –

Blessed are those who are invited to the

marriage supper of the Lamb". And he

said also, "These are true words of God".

[Rev 19:1-9 (Dn 12:12)]

CHAPTER FOURTEEN

FAITHFUL AND TRUE

And John saw heaven opened, and

behold, a White Horse and He who sat on

it is called Faithful and True.. He is King of

kings and Lord of lords.. and He treads the

great winepress of God. An angel stands

in the sun and summons all the birds of

midheaven (the predator birds who fly

higher than the little birds). And John saw

the beast and the kings of the earth and

their armies assembled to make war

against He who sat on the white horse,

and His army. And the (world) beast is

seized and the false prophet (white clad

118

wizard and his philosophy which changed the world) is seized and they are both thrown "alive" into the lake of fire which burns with brimstone (and oil?) [Rev 19:11-20]

There's a bit of irony here.. as these two thrown "alive" into the lake, are not "living" persons. And the rest were killed with the sWord (Truth) which comes from the mouth of Him who sits on the white horse. [Rev 19:21]

"The spirits of demons" (had gone forth) "gathering them together for the war of the great day of God, the Almighty. Behold I am coming like a thief. Blessed is the one who stays alert. And they gathered them together to the place called

Armageddon". [Rev 16:14,15,16]

"And behold, a white cloud and One like a Son of man sitting.. the harvest of the earth is ripe.. the hour to reap is come.. and He reaped the earth (gathering the fruit).. and another, an angel with a sickle, also swung his sickle to earth.. 'gather the clusters from the earth, because her grapes are ripe' ..so the angel gathered the clusters and threw them to the earth, into the wine press of God's wrath"/consequences. [Rev 14:14-18]

CHAPTER FIFTEEN

ETERNAL TREES / TABERNACLES

Upon the stage now, is a lone angel.
"He has a great chain, and the key to the
bottomless pit of the abyss, and he lays
hold of the dragon, the serpent of old,
who is Satan and the devil, and binds him
for a thousand years. He throws him into
the abyss, and shuts and seals it over
him, so that he will not deceive the
nations any longer, until the thousand
years are fulfilled, then he must be
released for a short time, and will deceive
the nations which are in the four corners
(directions) of the earth, to gather them

together, once again, for war". [Rev 20:1-3,7,8]

"Thrones are thrown down, and those that judge sit on them, and those that were killed for not worshiping the beast, have come to life and reign with Christ" along with the rest of the "first resurrection". But the "rest of the dead live not til the thousand years are ended". [Rev 20:4]

After the thousand years, the devil is loosed from the abyss for a short while, gathers the nations, and like the sand of the seashore, for number, they come up upon the breadth of the earth, and surround the camp of the saints, the beloved city, but fire falls down from

122

heaven upon them, and the devil who deceived them is thrown into the lake of fire and brimstone, the second *death*, where the beast and false prophet are. [Rev 20:7-10]

Then we see a Great White Throne and He who sits upon it, from whose Presence, heaven and earth fled away and no place is found for them. And now the small and the great (the rest of the dead at the second resurrection) stand before God and books are opened and the book of life is opened.. And death and the grave is thrown into the lake of fire, the second death [Rev 20:11,12]. "The last enemy to be abolished is death" [1 Corinthians 15:26].

After the second resurrection has

occurred, and after a long day/years of

examination (or "judgement") of all

history and every life, anyone whose

name is not found written in the pages of

the book of life (anyone found not

believing) will have a part in the lake of

fire, "the second death". [Rev 20:13-15]

But then the world is made new! There

is a new heavens and a new earth.. with

no seas separating the peoples. And the

Holy City, the New Jerusalem will come

down from heaven, and from God, to the

earth, and a loud voice from the Throne

says, "Behold! The Tabernacle" (Presence)

"of God is among men, and He will dwell

among them, and they shall be His

people, and God Himself will live among them! And He will wipe away every tear from their eyes; and there shall no longer be any death, nor crying, nor pain, nor suffering; for the first things have passed away." And He who sits on the Throne says, "Behold I make all things new." And we see the River of the Water of Life, clear as crystal, coming from the Throne of God and of the Lamb... watering all the earth with its radiance.. where each person, or family, will live freely "under their own vine" and fruit tree, and where "the bear will graze with the cow, and the lion will" (once more) "eat straw like the ox.." [Rev 21:1-5; 22:1-7; Micah 4:4; Isaiah 11:7; Genesis 1:30]

Postscript:

"Be wise as serpents,

Harmless as doves.."

   – Mt 10:16

"You will be universally hated...

brother will betray brother.. children against

parents... and have them put to death.."

      – Mk 13:12,13

   S.O.S. 8:14.......

www.ingramcontent.com/pod-product-compliance
Lightning Source LLC
Chambersburg PA
CBHW031857090426
42741CB00005B/532